# This Valley

# THIS VALLEY

New & Selected Poems
2003-2013

by Paul Neumann

QUERCUS REVIEW PRESS
MODESTO, CA
2013

**QUERCUS REVIEW POETRY SERIES, 2013**
Sam Pierstorff, *Editor*

Published by Quercus Review Press
Department of English
Modesto Junior College
*quercusreviewpress.com*

First Printing
Printed in the United States of America

Book design by Sam Pierstorff
Cover and author photos by Doug Holcomb

Printed on acid-free paper
10 9 8 7 6 5 4 3 2 1



ISBN-13: 978-0615873312
ISBN-10: 0615873316

Publications by Quercus Review Press (QRP) are made possible with the support of the Modesto-Stanislaus Poetry Center. A portion of the proceeds from the sale of this QRP book will benefit the Haven Women's Center of Stanislaus and creative writing scholarships at Modesto Junior College.

*For Pamela,*
*her loving-kindness and greatness of spirit.*
*She lives in every line.*

# CONTENTS

## ONE

## TWO

## THREE

# ONE

# This Valley

*for Bill*

Through the valley's haze one sees
the smear of houses, the strip malls
clustered on the sides of 99, the mass
of traffic on the freeway, speeding
past this fertile earth, the soil and seed
now capped by concrete parking lots.
Small wonder that our children feed on
megaplex dreams, a feast of awesome
action heroes, serial killers and the casual
cruelty of ingenious machines, no wonder
that they seek miracles more complex
than the green weeds pushing through
small cracks in the sidewalk or the white
buds on the trees in the spring. Tilling the
earth, my Irish friend once said, is like
taking the sacrament, and when we work
the ground, turn the soil and ready the seed,
we slow our fall from grace.

# Jack Tone Road

Driving through the last of this great valley,
I know that saving grace is in the soil, wet
clods of dense earth turned up by the tractor,
on farms which have been worked for generations,
family farms, we used to call them, before
high yields grew more alluring than husbandry.

There's a barn by the side of the road, crouched
in a field gone fallow, dusty brown planks now
weathered and worn, slumped over with age,
in a place where valley oaks once grew and now
give ground to parking lots and other pavement.
The barn survives in the seepage of tract homes.

Further on, near the city, the road widens and
the first strip mall materializes. Then another.
They say that the old are reluctant to change,
and perhaps so. I know only that now I turn north,
drive back up Jack Tone Road, unwilling to let go
just yet.

## Dark Blood

The heavy light of a summer day
here in the valley, dust rising from
the furrows as the workers wrapped
from head to foot in heavy clothes
against the sun bend to the hoe,
their floppy hats throwing shade
on hidden faces. They have been
here always, working the loose soil,
thinning the row crops, pruning the
grape vines, picking the fruit hanging
heavy in the trees and the strawberries
clustered low on the ground.

This might be another country, these
fields outside the city, and the hum in
the still, hot air a language unfamiliar.
Every year the workers make their way
to the labor camps outside Patterson,
the dented trailers slumped by the
orchards near Hughson or Hilmar.
At the end of the season they are gone,
the fields picked clean and the earth
lying fallow, a few empty fruit boxes
scattered at the edge of the dirt road.
Another year.

It is possible to travel through the valley,
on I-5 or one of the smaller county roads,
and see only the landscape: the formless
workers blurred by the blended green of
farmland, by the wide canal that snakes
below the western foothills, carrying the silver
line of water south. But in the air a thought
hangs like a dirt devil, caught in a swirl of
crops and calloused hands, palms split
to the blood, long days in the sun, wealth
wrung from the earth. Profit and penance.
What words to fill the margins?

# Godlight

When I was a child, I thought it was
the sunset over Carmel Bay because
my mother would stand for a moment
and marvel at the light gathering in the
west and bathing all the clouds in color.
She wouldn't speak, but the wonder in
her face showed the mystery that for a
brief time moved her beyond her quiet life.

Later, sitting in a bar in Reno, Nevada,
I thought it was the amber glow in
a glass of bourbon, reflecting the
profound sadness in my young life,
a brief suspension in the swirl of love that
so confused me. The moment caught me
by surprise, this chance to see the image
of a future despite the power of the loss.

Who among us has not been touched by
godlight? The light itself means little,
wherever it is found, but what it prompts
can be profound---the promise life was
always meant to hold, the still unclaimed
abundance we have never realized. The
leper is made whole, the cripple walks, our
lives for a moment cleansed and possible.

# California Dreamin'

Walking up the yellow hills in twilight,
tawny grasses rippling at the road edge,
I move through the last part of the valley
left to itself and not brought to ruin. A few
cows browsing on the sloping hillsides,
birdsong drifting in a scatter of oak trees,
field mice foraging in the fading light. And
why have I come here? Where else to turn
in this muddled California fantasy but to
Del Puerto canyon? The hawk sails in a thermal;
the snake stalks the field mouse and strikes.

Below, the oven of a Central Valley summer,
heat rising off the asphalt, a stifling haze
that blurs I-5, McDonald's and the mega-station
where the drivers gas and use the rest room,
super-size a soda then hit the on-ramp.
They're hurrying toward the fantasy of Vegas,
the delusion of cruise ships or an air-conditioned
shopping mall, the intoxication of porn sites,
the drunken violence of a party crowd, the cruel
luxury of indolence and entitlement. Up here,
above Del Puerto, godlight rests with the hawk.

# Balance

Difficult when I step from one
    year to another,
each bringing me closer to an
    end which was
once a vague shimmer in the
    distance, like a
mirage in the desert, but is now
    clear on the
horizon as the sun begins to set.

Of course, it is now that balance
    is so important:
one misstep on a slippery sidewalk,
    one fall from a
stool while reaching too high and
    then Prompt Care
to wait for a doctor and an even
    longer wait while
the broken bone heals and sets.

Sometimes it's not a bone that
    is broken, but a bond
with a child who has a heart you
    are sure you can
heal, so you stretch yourself
    further and higher
than you know you should,
    beyond the limits
that you and the child have set.

The young pay little for losing
    their balance: a few
bruises, a few scrapes, a new
    job, a new wife,
rehab, and some years to find
    firm footing. The
old lack that insolent prosperity
    so they try to hold
their ground as the sun sets.

# Carmel Lagoon

Say the egret in the raft of kelp,
fishing the vastness of the ocean,
was just a fragment of the life
I saw on the trail  near Carmel
Point. Like the sunset, like the
rhythms of the tide, like the rocks
standing sentinel over the sea-
surge, just a moment, caught,
as I walk toward the lagoon and
the swirls of seabirds clouding
the beach and the quiet water.

In a patch of grass, small island of
bright green in the larger conception
of the marsh, the duller sedge and
reeds, two yearling deer are thrusting
young antlers at young antlers, biding
their time until their appetite is fed
by the herd. All around me as I walk
is the sight and smell of life, the salt
in the air, the wave-spume above the
beach, the pelicans beginning their
awkward search above the sea.

And why have I come here? Not to seek
nor to find but to confirm my communion
with the force, the source of this harmony.
Some would say such a walk is useless,
that only theology can bridge the vastness
between God and man, but I know the
scatter of quail on the headland, the quick
movement of rabbits as they seek their
burrows, the endless circling flight of the
sea birds, climbing and falling in the sky
above the lagoon. The walk is the journey.

# Consolamentum

*for Pamela*

Only a faint gray light in the sky
this afternoon: the grasses on the bluff
above the ocean are flattened by the wind
and swirls of rain, the sea below me
roiled and confused. Six decades on this
earth and so little I have come to know.
I've been walking on a bluff above
a winter ocean, sometimes it seems,
all my life, looking for a way to parse
the moment when the storm clouds gather
and light appears to have left the sky,
but the air is always misty, the water far below.
Only when I turn home across the headland,
across the dunes to the woman I abide with,
does the arid grammar of uncertainty turn
into easy, flowing language I can live with.
In her I enter the fathomless ocean, diving
below the surface, riding the swell of the tide.

# Holding an Edge

is never easy, even when
support is firm and flexible,
and shock can be absorbed,
when fear is not a factor.

In the flat light, darkness
descending and shadows
on the snow, the run almost
over, care must be taken.

Falling can be so painful,
such a sudden discovery
of aging and its changes,
the clarity inescapable

But until that numb blow,
balance must be held on
every run, the body ready
and eyes always ahead.

## History Lesson

What I remember of the war's beginning
was my parents huddled by the yellow
eye of the radio, the ration cards, my
mother sewing blackout curtains, the
bacon fat my father used instead of butter,
him weeping in his room, the letter with
the foreign stamps so lifeless in his hands,
my mother comforting the aunt with the
older son, the one we couldn't talk about.
And yet, they say, those were the good old
days, when people left their doors unlocked,
a handshake sealed a business deal, and
that good war unified our nation. How hard
it is to understand a history when our parents
fashion memories meant to ease the exercise
of truth and leave their quiet lives unconfused.
My father never talked about the relatives he left
in Poland, and the suitcase filled with mother's
keepsakes stayed packed beneath her bed.

# Mortality

Late fall in the great valley
and the Chinese Pistache,
the Liquid Amber and Ginkos
are beginning to turn, a sharp
edge to the air this morning
when I walked the dogs.

A thin but brilliant sun hangs in
a low sky, heavy cluster of yellow,
orange and bronze leaves in
the street trees, and pangs of
light that pierce my slow eye,
last ache of summer ending.

Soon rain will fall on the quiet
streets, the first winds of winter
will blow the leaves into a scatter,
and they will rustle on the pavement
until the tires of passing cars turn
them to colorless mulch.

# High Tech Memory

In this dream of language,
I see the last image of my father,
taken on my eye-phone through
the window in the door of the ward
in the asylum and imported to
my heart-drive. I've photo-shopped
that memory, of course, cropped
the twisted, blue-grey legs and
the right arm thrust out toward
the looming male nurse. Of the
terror-stricken face, only the eyes
remain, deep and staring blankly.
In those pools I find my memories,
still keen and quick. His hand in
mine, we walk beside the ocean.
There is no closure, no cap on the
lens of grief. The file opens, again
and again, unbidden.

# Seasons' Change

Green fields striped with
dark brown furrows, the
dusty yellow leaves about
to drop as autumn fades,
last nuts knocked and
fallen, the rumble of a
harvester in a faraway field:
faint prayer.

As the
seasons change here in the
valley, there are no freezing
snaps or sudden shifts of
weather; the grape vines
turn each day toward death,
and first rains strip the fruit
trees bare.

When houses grow
like weeds in fertile fields, the
old world starts to slide into
disorder. In these early winter
days the wind is crisp and limbs
cast narrow shadows; the clouds
hang dark and low, and lightning
flickers in the air.

# The Difficulty with Poetry

Last night, at a dinner party,
a woman who knew I was
a poet asked what it was
that I wrote about. These days,
I said, commonly, I write
about death, and I was prepared
to go further down that rich and
precipitous path, to talk about
the great cycle of life, death
as a welcoming friend, even
the small death that is the
aftermath of sex, all that intricate
mystery. But she had already
grasped the handrail tight in her
gold-encircled hands and just said
"oh."

## This City

This city where I live, where
I will die, lies in a valley lush
with farmland: orchards, row
crops and vineyards from one
range of western foothills to
another in the east, the richest
land, some say, in the world,
watered by three great rivers.

Yet many, these days, mistake
modesty for mediocrity, wish
for more swagger and glitter,
a name in lights, the splash
and splendor that lure tour buses.
Is it only the old who can value
quiet comfort in the ordinary, find
wealth in the green bud's growth?

My father fled childhood poverty
in Poland, came here and worked
at anything. He never made a success
that could be measured, but he found
wonder in a warm bed, a chair in
the sun, saw godlight in every dinner
my mother made, every meal
a communion with simple virtues.

# Way Points

We left harbor in Vancouver, motored out
against the tide and set our way points for
a halfway mooring, cruising effortlessly
on a flat and featureless sea, checking radar
regularly, avoiding the minor irritation of an
occasional floating log on our steady way
through Active Pass and the channel still
ahead.

Eventually, we followed the headings to
Cowichan Bay: dark seawater rising, falling
against the pilings, a rusted trawler tied up
by the gas pump, seabirds riding on the water,
working the exhausted ocean, small boats
returning empty to the harbor in the fog,
steering only by the fading lights on a bleak
shore.

When we set the way points and calculated
the headings, we could not predict how the nature
of a mooring would alter our perspective. We left
Cowichan Bay at early light, cruising easily away,
but people were already stirring. There were nets
to be mended, lines unsnarled, boats to be rigged
in the cold damp air: the exercise of necessary
labor.

# Weather Report

Foggy this morning. A gray memory holds off the sun.
From the bluff I watch my children play on the beach,
burrowing deep in the yielding sand, digging for treasure.
The foghorn sounds like a fading pulse, clouded and flat.

When I was a child, my father would walk each morning
in summer to the sea wall, sit on this bench beside me,
stare at the ocean through deepening mist, watching waves
breaking on the bar and dying, finally, in the sand.

Father you were comfortable in the fog those last days.
Mother and I, we caught your jabber, slicked your skin,
wiped the brown gravy from your slack wet mouth.
Finally there was no sound, no reason not to take you.

Now, when I sit by the sea with my sons, I look for the great
shark to show his terrible fin, for the rogue wave to scour the sand,
for you to return, Father, to ask why you shriveled away left
alone, at Agnews, naked in the white glare of florescent lamps.

# Of God and Faith at Carmel Point

Rain clouds are massed at the head of the valley,
ominous and gray, while thin sunlight falls through
scattered clouds and I walk slowly on a trail above
the ocean toward the Carmelite Monastery, the place
where I was taught with such certitude about God:
His will: our peace.

Today, twenty children, seven others, were cut down
by a crazed gunman in a kindergarten in Connecticut,
and the mystery begins to unfold for the parents and
townspeople, the sudden emptiness in their lives, the
depth of the abyss, the desperate need for a reason,
any kind of sense.

As I walk, I think how slippery a fish is faith, so
lovely in the mind of a child, so difficult to hold firm
as we age. In the sky, the clouds form a monstrous
shape, and sunlight casts yellow light that turns orange,
purple, red as the sun settles slowly in the west and
sinks into the horizon.

# Here in the Valley

The jobs young people used to do
have passed away: grading peaches
in the sheds, picking tomatoes off
the vine, irrigating all night with a spade
and a six-pack, the water gushing
in the thirsty furrows.

Now they work inside a fast-food
outlet, taking orders, punching
prices into a computer, handing out
sacks of tasty fat and salty fries,
super-sizing the drinks: a minimum
wage to feed the car.

Livy once said that the Roman Empire
fell when its people stopped tending
their land, preferring to live in the city
for its banquets and lush idleness. But
who reads Livy anymore? At school we
watched the video.

# Sex in my Seventies

There is still the undulating surface
of the sea, pulsing with sudden force,
and a tidal surge that sucks against
the shingle, foams, then dies on the
yielding sand.

We have said these words before,
moaned our pleasure like a fading wind.
This private place, this cove below the
bluff on Carmel Point, is always sheltered
from the storms.

In the random wildness of our younger
years, we would visit this place often,
reckless and sure this blessing would
be always ours, aware of the fragility
but heedless and assured.

Now, in my seventies, I am less certain
and wonder if I will come this way again,
my heart full but my body a cloud of godwits,
wheeling and unsettled as the sun sets
slowly in the west.

# Aging

The light is fading in the west.
Only the highest branches of the pines
still hold the sun. We sit on the deck,
you and I, at peace in our chairs,
and watch the last brilliance of the day
begin to dim into shadowy night.

Can you feel the weight of these words,
the gravity pulling our sun toward
the horizon? But if summer were endless,
would we value this last light,
this glow in the tops of the trees,
the memory of this evening in the fall?

# The Body Politic

My wife says that my body is changing,
          trousers slack
in the rear, buttocks frail and formless,
          the flesh falling
away, the deficit uncontrollable. Now

          it's just a matter
of waiting for The Big One: heart attack,
          cancer, the fiscal
cliff or another war. There's nothing further
          to be done,
resolutions made and enacted: all that

          biking and walking,
a careful diet, but no way now to govern
          a body falling slowly
into decline. It does not seem so long ago
          that the state
of my body was sound, several surgeries

          to be sure,
but always the muscles regaining their tone
          and tension.
Now this gradual recession, and no renewal
          seems possible,
every glance in the mirror a reflection of the loss.

## Reading the River

*for our forty-first anniversary*

The rivers in the valley begin in the Sierra
when a warming spring brings snowmelt,
and tiny rivulets become creeks and streams.
flowing down the long sides of the mountains.
Those first waters, high in the Sierra, are also
the most perilous: wild cascades, rocks and
strainers; even eddies swirl with abandon, and
the snowmelt runs wild in narrow channels.

Finally, the wild waters run their course and
flow into the broad brown rivers of the valley,
carrying silt and a quiet salvation. Who knows
where passion might otherwise end? But even
when the river has spread and moves easily in
its bed, subtle currents can lead to snags and
hidden rocks. A careful reading of the river can
sometimes take the lifetime of a marriage

before it flows into the sea.

# Happy Families

Many of my friends have happy
          families, so
they say, children prosperous
          and settled,

grandchildren bright and gifted:
          Tim's on
scholarship at college, Jill an
          intern at

some startup in the city. They
          are fluent
in foreign languages, play the violin
          or piano,

do community service projects in
          third world
countries, manage their money
          and avoid

unfortunate commitments. They
          all vacation
on the coast together every year.
          Is it my

imagination that these family stories
          seem so
incomplete, some pages missing or
          withheld?

# California, California

The first cold wind of autumn,
and dry leaves are rustling on
the street. The sun hangs low,
and early darkness is looming.
But crops are in, and Wal-Mart
full. What need for moderation?
Why not indulge ourselves? So
my friend said, let's max the
cards, vacation in Vegas, some
shit like that, he said. The night's
still young, I said, why wait for
tomorrow? Whatever, I said. Get
in the car. I'll drive.

# Here

Outside my kitchen window,
in the riot of red bougainvillea,
I hung a seed bag for the finches,
and I watch them work, while
I wait for the water to boil
for my tea.

In the distance, I can hear
the sounds of the highway,
thousands of cars, translating
men and women who think
if they hurry they'll make the life
they wish for.

In a French village, years ago,
I learned the virtue in waiting,
how much can be seen when
time stands still and the eye
is slow, how even small birds
can spread seeds.

# Lobos

An evening at Lobos, light
golden on the sea stacks,
fog swirling in wisps of grey.
In the parking lot, a woman
with a cigarette sprawled
in her mouth, and tattoos
covering thighs and legs,
a nasal voice snarling her
boredom.

In this nightmare of language,
a monstrous future shudders
out of the looming darkness
and squats near the parked
cars, sniggering at piercings,
smokes and tats, graffiti and
gangsta rap: the casual cruelty
of mindless intrusion and selfish
entitlement.

Then ocean and sky, the wind
and waves, pine and cypress,
as the evening unfolds, move
to manage that gross shape,
consume it with the constantcy
of Point Lobos, a place of mist
and godlight, sustained by the
trees and the tidal sway of
the sea.

# Of Whales and Marriage at Point Sur

The whales migrate through the sunless ocean,
moving in pods but solitary, steering their course
through the depths by instinct, an occasional sound
going out from one through the fathomless sea to another,
the song from Scammon's Lagoon echoing through
the vast and lonely waters, then berthing like a heartbeat
in leviathan deep in the chasm of the Monterey Canyon,
a delicate resonance, a slender chord, that still haunts me.

In 1995, remember, we stood at the side of our son's bed,
his head in bandages, the doctors silent. My eyes met yours
somewhere in the quiet depths of that room. How close we
came to the edge of ruin, but something passed between us,
some great form nosing through that sea of cloudy fear,
finning through the murky water. When we blinked, then
looked away, motes of dust swirled in the damp air, golden
in the sunlight. Our son awoke and asked for ice cream

# The Pelicans as Poets at Carmel Point

From the bluff below the cross
I see them idling on the lagoon,
fitfully splashing at the water
with their great white wings or
rising awkwardly into the sky
then dropping suddenly back
into the shallows, just aimlessly
entering the air and then the water.

But see them fly as the glowing
gathers in the west and godlight
is all that can be seen on the horizon.
Watch as they glide above the bay,
above the waves and search the water,
wings held and soaring, roaming
the surface of the mystical depths,
fishing what the ocean discloses.

# Sidney Spit

We woke this morning moored
off Sidney Spit, a long tongue
of sand just off the Gulf Islands,
some shafts of sunlight slanting
through the gray skies and mist.
All yesterday we beat against
the wind and rain, growling through
troubled water and ran in, finally,
to this mooring, relieved, drank
white wine, ate spot prawns and
slept warm and dry in down bags:
complacent, indolent and secure..

Now, the boat rocks on an early
morning swell, and a man in a
weathered fishing boat close by
pulls up a rusted wire trap, throws
handfulls of stunted crabs back into
the dark water, keeps the only one
or two he can sell, turns hopefully
toward the next trap and hungers
in the morning light for a miracle
to come walking across the water.

# Evangelists

It is Sunday in the valley, late springtime
and the miracle of budding almond trees,
greening grapevines and the luxurious
spread of lupine and poppies across the
range of foothills in the east: April, Easter,
and the resurrection of the earth from the
chill tomb of winter.

Soon lambs will play in the meadows, fish
will rise in the warming San Joaquin, the
great cycle will begin again, renewing our
faith despite the fragility: the falling of the
spirit as the sun fades in the west; the cloak
of night; the pause before dawn light appears,
then the shining wonder.

In the mega-churches, the pastors preach
God's word to confident congregations, rich
with certainty. The evangelists know the
density of human failing, the specific gravity
of repentance, the speed of prayer as it
arcs upward, the path the rich must take
to enter heaven.

The words of Jesus are parsed each week
at bible study, then phrased again for true
believers who settle in the Sunday pews,
hungry for good news. There are buildings
to be funded, the poor to be pitied, no need
to doubt the certain order of creation or
marvel at its mystery.

# The Old Mill Cafe

This is the height of summer in the valley,
tawny grasses trampled down and burnt to
straw, a few faded flowers still struggling
to live in quiet shade away from the sun
and its searing heat..

At a table in the Old Mill Cafe, the men
gather each day for  coffee and stories,
their faces lined with the memories of war
and the wear of hard work, plain men with
calloused hands.

They are the grandsons of Okies, sons
of the hard West Side, and they talk about
the Mexicans who take the jobs that their
children will not do: pulling cotton south
of Corcoran:

using short hoes in the fields near Turlock:
picking peaches on hot, dusty summer days.
No small farms are left in the Great Valley,
only food stamps and welfare, minimum wage.
No decent jobs.

On the West Side, yards filled with weeds,
rusted cars in the driveway, swamp coolers
in the windows, a geranium in a cracked pot
for the child, quickened by school, who moved
away, never to return.

# Walking the Urban Trail

This early summer sun has browned
the native grasses, turned them pale yellow.
The seed pods sway in the wind on slender
stalks, and the green force is almost gone.
But there are secrets here that only a slow
eye can see; a ceanothus crouched among
the brown foxtails, a blue so piercing that
it almost blinds.

While I walk the trail, indifferent drivers
pass the wealth that lies beside the road.
Rushing, hurrying in their cars, they have
business to do, money to make, places to go.
No time for black-eyed susans rising up from
the tawny grass, no time for the burst of lupine
spread like wine stains in the tangle. These
mysteries will never slow them.

# Of Rodrigo and God in Steamboat

Walking down Elk Lane toward River Road
and the western slope of the Rockies, the
sounds of the Rodrigo Concierto de Aranjuez
still play, over and over, in my mind. Last
night, the music rolled out of the guitar and
the orchestra and from His mouth down the
valley, past the mountains, and flowed with
the river.

Haven't we all heard a melodic line
so lovely that it lingers in the mind, a tune so
haunting that we think we have heard the voice
of God or the consoling sounds of love? When
we look up at a mountain range or see a river
clear on stones or a crimson sunset in the sky,
stunned by those visions, don't we find an
order in our scattered lives?

Along River Road,
the music still rolling in my mind, I see reed
green, tree green. sage green, grass green,
bush green and above the road the rise of green
Mt. Werner, all those subtle and distinctive
shades combining to form the harmony of the
valley, its river and mountains and the fathomless
skies of His love.

# TWO

# Soter*

In the green time, in spring, in
the valley, those who would
seek the savior will find Him
in the fields where the water
rushes in to soften the earth
and dark clods are disgorged
by the turning of the plow.
At rest from his work, the
farmer kneels in the furrows,
fingers the soil and knows
his land, knows there is no
miracle more sacred than
the rise of seeds through
earth to the air, the growth
of green leaves on the trees,
the promise of blossoms, the
radiant mystery of the land
in deep bloom, random and wild.

** an ancient synonym for the savior*

# Carmel Afternoon

As a child, the fading gold of afternoon was dusty,
yellowed light on crocheted doilies covering
every arm of easy chair and sofa, piano silent
in the corner, rosewood cover closed. The endless
talk of adults lingered in the stale air like smoke,
and I would make my way alone to walk the beach.

This afternoon, now in my middle years, I am lying
with you in a glow of sunlight, a golden shining on
a mass of silken sheets and pillows, the rhythm
of the waves sounding in the distance, an insistent
force that breaks, then curls toward shore, as we lie
still entwined and listen to Mozart on the stereo.

What brought us to this afternoon in Laurel Cottage?
The golden sun is setting through the wooden shutters,
evening is approaching, and our place is in the kitchen,
heating dinner or watching television in the easy chairs.
But when you stroked my hand and then my arm,
the dusk receded, and we climbed lightly up the stairs.

# A Runner's World

On Monday he straddled the back of the wind,
rode out and in, one long breath held,
his body home before his mind awakened.

Tuesday, he slowly waded in a tide pool,
watched the scuttling crabs in their swirling
world, rubbed his fingers on a starfish.

The way on Wednesday seemed to lead inside.
The land was unfamliar; frightened,
he lay beneath a tree beside a girl
who was his mother, his daughter, his wife.

Thursday, he filled a silver chalice with his blood
drank it down, slumped to the ground,
murmurring, exclaiming,
savoring the taste remaining on his tongue.

Friday, he could only take one step. It took
forever. He could not move the stones that were his feet,
nor could the hand that was his heart push
the stiffened leather bag that held his breath.

On Saturday he was alone.
It was a stretch of desert that he wandered,
unafraid, listening to the lizards stir the sand,
the dry slither of hunting snakes.

Sunday was ripe and plump to bursting.
Afterward, relaxing at the antique oaken table,
he carved a nectarine, bit cleanly through the skin
then pulpy flesh. The juice ran down his chin.

# 9/11

When the terrorists attacked, we were in Maine
with friends, about to fly to France, and we
woke to the news, watched the towers fall
and survivors flee while rescuers died and
the commentators wondered how and why.
That evening on the deck I stared out at old-
growth pines and maples, imagined shadows
stalking through trees, the flash of axe on flesh
and the randy swirl of native rage.

The oldest stories lie in the mind like stones
buried deep in the ground, so my friend said
when he used the remnants of an old rock wall
to build a fireplace at his house: quarry stones,
river stones, found stones, survivals from the wall
that had civilized his land and could only come alive
when the fire had been lit, the logs consumed in
flames, the embers turned so hot that the old stones
glowed in sullen anger.

What country has not been touched by terror?
We all carry scars of old wounds, proud flesh that burns
when stories are told by the fire and stones glow
in the heart. For days now I have thought about
America, America, the imperial tolling of that iron
bell, our towers of steel and concrete rising up from
blood-stained ground, the embittered hubris of this
great country, the arrogance we cannot acknowledge,
the absolution that we hope for.

## Games of Chance

No higher stakes than love, of course.
In the old days the slot machine handles
were hard to pull, three cherries slow
to line up; you had to work to try your
luck: head to a bar, get a blind date,
ask a friend to find your love. Now, the
wheels spin electronically, without any
effort, all computerized: E-Harmony,
Christian Mingle, Match.com. Couples
are created if profiles seem compatible
and online photos look attractive. Still
long odds on a happy marriage, however.
The jackpot bars have to fall in place
and stay there, no matter what, or else
an empty coin cup.

# Eggs

White. Ovoid.
Light in the hand yet heavy with promise.
They press in my palm with grave insistence.
My fingers know their fragility, sense the potency
held in the shell, the fine-walled asylum, shadowed sanctuary,
the opaque dance of conception veiled in a particulate cloud.
China white. Or mottled brown. Warm in the nest
but cool in my hand as I close the refrigerator door,
place the skillet on the stove, add a nut of butter,
taste of salt and pepper to the pan.

I take my morning eggs overeasy, a buttery film
holding the embryonic form. With the first thrust of the fork,
the white albumen is streaked with curls of yolk, then it swirls
across the open space of the plate like a great nebula,
like the lacy whirl of the Milky Way, or the froth of a dying wave,
shorebirds picking the small crabs from the foam.

# Common Prayer

In the old *retalbo* I see the form of my grandson
and his mother, simple figures outlined on a sheet
of tin with a prayer of supplication or gratitude
scrolled clumsily below. In Berkeley, years ago,
We talked of family, fatherhood, fidelity, a smear
of abstract words. Unbelievers, none of us had ever
comforted a failing parent, known the terror of
bronchitis, or the taste of coffee when a wife says
she is leaving with another man and she is sorry,
the emptiness of that drained cup. None of us had
ever known the labor that is love, the toil of marriage,
the intrictate knots that bind a family, the conflicts
faithless words can cause, the distinct fragility
of every moment. In the *retalbo*, there is an angel
sending grace in a golden stream from heaven.
How else to lighten the shadow over all our lives?

## Growing Up

I was with my aging father at a party,
when he disappeared behind a curtain
with a clutch of drunks who wanted,
I thought, to see snow light the dark air
as it fell silently and gracefully down.
A moment later he emerged, red-faced
and stumbling, followed by an angry
woman, her blouse in disarray, saying
nothing, of course, leaving the child to
wonder what might have been revealed.

# Thinking of Mladic* and Marriage

Years ago, in Serbia, Mladic's
army herded men and boys into
barns, burned some alive, shot
the survivors, forced the women
into shame, a randy burst of rage.
A cleansing, he called it, but the
people survived the violence and
lived on.

Today, the wild grasses turned
to straw, a city crew came out to
weed the urban trail, cutting stalks
before the seed can germinate and
choke another generation of lupine,
tidy tips and golden poppies, the
wild flowers so well-loved, but the
grasses will abide.

Tonight I lie with the woman I love,
her hair a pale yellow on the pillow.
The urgency of our bodies has quieted,
our seed already ripened, the fruit
of a long germination. The green fuse
flowered in us without the curse of
violence and found the way to further
generations.

**Radko Mladic was a Serbian general,
indicted for war crimes by the Hague.*

# With My Son at Elkhorn Slough

1

Fifty years ago, Sage, we would have come here to hunt.
Father and son: fog hanging on the margins of the land;
trees submitting to the early morning mist. Out in the shallows,
decoys strung in a careful line, drops of water beading
their backs, as the sun breaks through the fog in pale shafts.
When the first ducks dive toward water and land in a rush,
we rise, you and I, thrust up our steel guns and shoot and shoot,
our thunder drowning the quiet morning and the birds' weak cries.
Then I smear blood on your cheeks and hug your shoulders. Hard.
That night, back home, you cruise McHenry, and I spread the legs
of your mother. Father and son. The exhausted customs of love.

2

Today in our sea kayaks we lie low in the water, flow up the slough
on the fetch of the tide, paddling and sweeping in rhythm with
the pull of the moon. We nose up creeks on the rising waters
near murres and egrets; long-billed curlews and whimbrels stare
from the grass-covered shoreline. Out on the estuary, we glide past
pods of young white pelicans with orange bills. They stretch their wings,
rise off the water, settle again as we pass by. Our voices soft, our
paddles feathered, we are sometimes almost close enough to touch.

# First Death

A winter storm blew through last night,
this morning fallen limbs on the street,
buds shorn from the pear trees and
a bitter chill in the air as I walk the dog.

This week I lost the first of my circle
of friends, not to the riotous spread
of cancerous cells or a bolt in the heart,
just the last storm in a long winter.

When the cold wind descends on a friend
the same age, then your own clouds darken,
and you move more carefully, facing the
lidless, staring eye and your fragile life.

As a boy in church, listening to the words
of the priests, I was terrified by the awful
immensity of the infinite, the black hole
yawning. Now I walk while the seasons
turn.

# Coming of Age

The steady set of winter storms
has stripped the beach to bedrock,
and the fine white sand where children
play in summer has washed away.

But the weathered stone remains,
though worn by wind and wave,
and I wade each day in the surf looking
out toward the deepest waters.

# The Old Ball Game

It's the last of the seventh and the starting
pitcher is still in. He has good velocity and
a sharp break on the curve, but he misses
his spots, occasionally, and he seems to
be tiring.

The set-up man, in the bullpen, has been
steady all year. The eighth inning is always
his, and he throws strikes, low and away
on the corners, has great command and
no one ever walks.

The closer is a mystery; you never know
what to expect. He starts you out with two
fast balls, taken for strikes, then a slider
with a break you can't read. Weak swing.
ICU. Game over.

# New Growth

*for Megan*

This morning, staring at the dot of dark blood
in the corner of my newly-bitten nail, I see
my father's eye, my mother crouched and crying,
shadows of the past, as I will be a shadow for you.
Last night I lay beside you as you groped for sleep.
"Are there tigers underneath my bed?" you asked me.
Impatient, I gave you an adult's reply. Today,
my love, I am crying as I write these words,
so fearful are those tigers and so stained with blood.

# Regime Change

All day this emptiness,
the valley waiting for the winter storm,
birds wheeling and scattering in the sky,
a whirl of leaves fluttered to the ground.
No rain. And the nervous earth on edge.
Finally, as the earth tilts toward midnight,
black clouds muster, the wind begins
to howl, and a hard rain assaults the soil.

What comes with the rain? What seeds will be
sown by the wind? What will rise to replace
old patterns of trees and shrubs, the scatter
of valley oaks, deep rooted, set firm in random
places on the hillsides? Will there be new
bushes and saplings to hold the soil in place?
Or a riot of plants in disorder, unable to stop
the slide until it dies at the bottom of the canyon?

In Palm Springs, there is little rain, no change
of season. The golfers pass the day from
tee to green and home again to the soft glow
of the barbeque, the thin gleam of the TV screen,
the company of neighbors who turned their
field crops into fortunes and work no more.
After drinks they eat their dinner while coyotes
howl in mountains high and arid as Afghanistan.

# Exploration

Some say old men
should be explorers,
moving out, unafraid,
from the quiet shores
of their lives, away,
eyes on the horizon.
After all, what is there
to lose?

But if we want to take
a measure of our lives,
of our merit and meaning,
then exploration in the
twilight must go inside,
without guides, only
cryptic marks on the
unused map.

There's not much time
left, after all, a few quiet
moments for checkers
or loving grandchildren.
The clock ticks; a life
is either explored at the
end or settles like dust
in the darkness.

# Tao

For me, a way is living
at the edge of ruin, while
mindful of the moment's
fragility. Even as I age,
I climb the steep path
above the creek. In the
tension between skin
and blood, the scarp of
mountain and the flowing
water, meaning lies.

On the boat between two
lives, foreign and wordless,
my father fought with men
who tried to rob him: bone
on bone, skin and blood. He
kept his money and docked
in New York harbor, but that
passion never left him, though
he found a way that harbored
pain and finally led to peace.

# Amigos Nadando

*for Dan and Jim*

Into the pool of a metaphor, I watch you dive.
Arms outstretched, heads bent, you begin to swim
with awkward strength and thrashing power, telling
your watery beads, one by one, stroke by stroke,
lap by lap: mutilated desaparecidos, young men
sharing a needle, vaporized Japan, the liberal rosary.
At the end, your legs hardly kick, your arms barely pull.
You gasp at the ladder, exhausted. Then I see you
shouldering out of the pool, droplets of water falling
to the ground, and you stand in sunlight. Always,
in this dream of language, I see you last in sunlight.

Amigos nadando, quienes nadan por ti

# Regeneration

Recovering from surgery, I walk each day
down the Virginia Corridor, an urban trail
bordered in native valley grasses, yarrow,
California poppies, purple owl clover, blue
flax, and lupine: random bursts of color.
My friends commiserate: your fourth surgery
and at your age. I point to the green weeds
forcing through the cracks in the concrete.
Against all the odds. The celebration.

# Bad News

When the letter arrived or the telephone
rang or you stood in the doorway stunned
with the newspaper in your hand, there
was a bewildered moment before the
stone was thrown into the pond and the
ripples began their rhythmic movement
out toward the shore of grief. You know
how your insides flex and knot against
bad news? How you stoop to brace yourself
against the shock of that first ripple? How
your muscles cannot hold themselves so
they quiver and shake? Bad news is a wound
that never fully heals: the newborn baby's
withered hand, a sudden death, the bracing
fracture of divorce. Your proud flesh smarts
whenever it is even slightly touched.

# Barr-Epstein

Yesterday, the rapture of the summer
sun was everywhere on Carmel beach:
a scatter of children digging in the sand,
dogs chasing through the smaller waves
and surfers riding heavy swells to shore.

Today, a tongue of fog moves slowly
up the Carmel River mouth, extends
across the headland just below the
cross at Yankee Point and covers all
the bay from Lobos to Stillwater Cove.

Above the fog, blue sky and sunlight, but
today this clinging coastal mist I walk
through on the empty beach in silence.
"The pathogen is nothing," said Pasteur,
explaining illness. "Terrain is everything."

As a boy, alone and playing in the twisted
cypress branches by our home, I saw monsters
in the fog, some gloomy creatures I could not
escape and once a swarthy bear that stalked me.
My mother told me I was seeing things.

## Fracture

Not a crack on the MRI, no
        crooked ridge,
sharp break or jagged split
        just a dark
flaw, a caesura in the seamless
        length of

my fifth metatarsal, persistent
        pain, my
foot encased in a clumsy boot.
        There can
also be a fracture in a family,
        hurt feelings,

lingering resentment, awkward
        avoidance,
moments when eyes are averted,
        silence
smolders. Some fractures can be
        accidental,

a careless step or random slight.
        You can
live with a fracture in the foot, but
        in a family
if there is no regret, no spoken
        offer to

mend the break and rebuild the
        balance,
then healing can be long, the
        offended
member cast in sullen silence, no
        reunion.

# Calypso

*for Pam*

1

This steady house rests among hills formed like women,
long tawny flanks flowing down to creeks and streams,
slopes in silhouette beneath the darkling sky this evening,
canyons holding the last blue light as the wind begins to rise.

Sheltered in the house, I turn to the body of the woman I love,
trust my thighs to her clasp, feel our movement in my marrow.
After, our bodies spread like wine stains on the rumpled sheets,
and we sleep entwined as the purple sky opens.

2

Does the steady rain enter the ardent earth? Does the soil
alter to manage the slow submission of falling water?
Or does the headlong flood flash past hills and slopes
in a vain rush and spend itself before it reaches the sea?

I have been that way before, lost in a storm of wild wind,
beaching my van on some insular shore, transient, searching,
where a woman would fuck my breath away in a frenzy
and send me off to try again and again.

3

This morning, in sunlight, we walked the hill near the house,
your fingers wound in my hair, my arm encirling your waist.
The green canopy of the forest shaded the sky, and the sun
dropped shafts of light through the moisture-laden air.

We walked among worn trunks of trees grown together,
a grove of old-growth redwoods where a scatter of orchids
burst through the dark brown mulch of the seasoned ground
in random spells of color, as luminous as a long marriage.

# Divorce

The day the first rains came
the baby cried, the dog tracked
wet marks on the kitchen floor,
and we found things to do
in separate rooms.

All winter there were dull gray
clouds and steady drizzle, damp
we could not escape and so
in March you moved into your
own apartment.

In the first few years, a marriage
opens with a form of love, a fashion
which may not survive a change
of season, or the ache and pain of art.
So then divorce.

# Entering the Seventies

It was like Beethoven arriving at Mortonvassar,
huddling in the carriage, obsessive, half-blind,
about to enter the service of the spoiled princess.
There was white chiffon and sunlight on the sofas,
gold-flecked accents on the damask-covered chairs.
A hundred peacocks wandered through the garden
amid the pungent scent of careless, wanton pleasures.
I was driven up, stepped slowly out the door and felt
the electricity; shaken, I murmured to the force that
fetched me, “Breaking, I am breaking on this shore.”

## Habit

My mother worried about my lack of
structure, my inability to plan,
the absence of consistency.

But now, these days, I hold tight to
habits and do what I have come
to expect, the usual routines

that have become the way I make a
life---so the walks each day
on the trail and the food I eat

moderately in the morning and the
evening and the wine I drink
indulgently at night are the lines

that mark my life as well as the books
I read and the words I write
to give shape to my thoughts.

But with the woman I love, there is no
force of habit. When the moon
is high in the summer sky,

communion moves in random ways,
and we travel, body and blood,
toward the edge of the horizon,

where the last flash of the sun lingers
for a second, then vanishes
into the western ocean and

only a glow, a scattering of light in the
sky and on the sea, remains.

# Phone Call

My granddaughter calls from LA,
eleven years old and thinking about
piercings, tattoos and studs, the
surface wealth of body art. Choices.
She has already been pierced by
her father's early death, tattooed
by her mother's last three live-in lovers.
A stud? That will surely come. What
words can I find to fill in the holes, to
cover the scars? And the stud---what
to say in warning about him, lurking
already in the corridors at school,
about to ask her to parties and other
confusions.

# Reading King Lear in La Quinta

Beneath the stark Santa Rosa mountains,
in the midst of a desert, this lush resort:
gated communities within gated communities,
estates preserved then passed to children:
wealth carved by the will while lawyers parse
the language of the dead, and the evil sisters
whisper in the ears of the bitter siblings.
There is bickering about the porcelain collection,
the ranch near Corcoran, the diamond solitaire
the mother always wore. America. America.
And Cordelia? My father left me a signet ring,
a thousand memories and a way to make a life.
No taxes due on the heart's abundance.

# Sitting with my Grandson

*for Carter*

It is dark where we are:
a cloud has crossed the
sun, and momentarily
our world is shaded, and
goblin heads rule. This is
the scary time when we
sit together close while
a cold wind blows, and
the flowers lie flat.

If we turn toward the sea,
turn our eyes to the west,
the world is open, and sun
is sparkling on the waves.
The horizon is limitless,
and blue sky bends down
to meet blue water. Carter,
you will always have to choose
which way you look.

The scariest goblins will try
to gnaw at your grown-up life
but only if you let them. In
the surf on Maui, remember
the sneaker waves that caught
us unaware and scared us?
On your worst days, when the
ocean rises up like an angry wall,
keep your dolphin smile.

# Sunday

We spent the day waiting for rain,
the whole of Sunday waiting for rain.
All day the storm was held offshore
by constant high pressure in the air.
The threat of rain stalled our resolve,
suspended all our planned activity.
Waiting for rain, we looked at the sky
through the living room windows,
watched white turn gray, then gray
turn dark until finally in the black of night,
Sunday was no more.

                                        Some days,
my father used to say, are like that,
days when you wait, it seems, a lifetime
for something to happen, but it never does.
Then your day has been misplaced. Lost
days we call those, or lost lives: days
when we think that whatever we do will be
ruined by rain, so we wait and do nothing.
To lose a day is easy, especially when
what we have to do is so difficult. But to find
a day again, my father used to say, to find
that day again is impossible.

# Ways of Death

A grey, damp fog this morning,
and expected to last some time.
In the night a hard rain fell,
hammered my windows, pelted
the walkway then stopped.

Last week the old neighbor died.
he would sit in his backyard and
watch the day fade. Turning in,
he fell. His children found him
in the morning when they came.

My mother died in a nursing home.
Tranquilized, her fragile heart held
many years more than it was meant to.
Eight years in a wheelchair. Cleaned
and fed, unable to see through the fog.

# Daughter

My best words for you always stayed
in my throat, and then I passed them
through my fingers to your hair. You
sat on my lap and bounced on my knee.
"This is the way the ladies ride: walk,
walk walk."

In the distance, your horses restive
by the river, velvet muzzles nosing roiled
water, muscles rippling bunched and
ready for the gallop that would take you
headlong to the moon.

Soon my touch became an imposition,
and so I used an ache of words, a torment
of advice, you would not hear. You sat in
someone else's lap and bounced and bounced.
This is the way the cowboys ride: gallopy,
gallopy, gallopy.

# THREE

# A War Story

*as told by Terry*

Mixed with my shit
were forty-three kernels
(I counted them later.)
of coarse brown rice
which I washed through
my fingers in the small cold
stream, and I ate the rice
squatting, in the mud, in Korea,
and I knew what war
can never mean to presidents,
generals, politicians, pollsters,
and middle-aged men.

Grunt---youngman---grunt

# Afternoon on the Yampa

In the valley of the Yampa,
the wheat has been cut,
gathered into yellow wheels
and left on the shorn ground.
The harvester has been retired,
stands abandoned in the field,
and the time for work is done.

Fall is the season to settle,
before autumn turns winter
and trees lose their leaves,
time to gather the harvest,
store our fortunes, retire to
the safety of our burrows,
guard against the unexpected.

But here, on the Yampa,
a fisherman casts a fly while
the light drains from the day.
He casts again and again
in the face of darkness and death,
catching and releasing, never
tiring in the twilight of his life.

# Arles

The sun was out today in Arles,
a heavy expanse of light weighing
on the tranquil order of the village.
All day the *mistral* added to the heat,
moaning through the plane trees and
winding down the quiet street
where I sat and drank black coffee
in a commonplace cafe, with people
passing by my table and morning
newspapers blowing in the doorway.

I thought of Van Gogh when he lived
here, choosing colors in his madness,
the whirling slash of his manic brush
across the canvas, the crazed light
in his eyes when he walked through
the mundane village, wild for love, the

impossible passion of a brittlecone pine
twisting through the hard Sierra granite.

# Avignon

In the hot sun before the Palace of the Popes,
we heard the sound of the guitar, first a Bach
prelude, flowing over the worn stones like a truth
you've always known, then some salsa and reggae,
Yanni and Elton John to amuse the milling crowd
below the silent walls whose smooth expanse held
back the molten sea of light and lines of tourists
waiting to enter the cool sanctuary where popes
dispensed indulgences and parsed the humble faith.

It is always thus. The simple words of Christ, whether
caught in music or carried in the form of a cathedral,
are ever cloistered from the vulgar multitude who gather
in the plaza with guide books, cameras, ice cream cones.
The Bach flows through and past the gaping crowd
who stand in wonder at the jugglers and the mime,
white-clothed and still who makes no movement,
makes no sound, until a coin is dropped into his bowl,
and then he whirls and bows. The crowd applauds.

# California Autumn

1

Up here in the Sierra, men came today
to cut the dead trees down around the cabin,
the dry pines invaded by hordes of beetles
commuting from tree to tree, forest to forest,
entering the bark, girdling the heartwood
and the trees slowly dying, needles falling
from shriveled branches, runnels of red pitch
staining the trunks. All morning rasp and whine
of chain saws split the quiet air, neighbors
spoke uneasily of draught, and the heavy thump
of toppled pines rumbled in the ground like a tocsin,
thunderous and deep. California. California.

2

Down below in the desert valleys, sun sparkles
on the swimming pools, sprinklers water the
the golf courses, the lawns, the beds of ornamental
flowers. There is a tinkle of ice in frost-beaded glasses,
a tumble of spray from the shower heads. A tanned
young man and woman stand and stare into the darkness
beginning to enfold the purple mountains. This September
sun has held them all day long in the air-cooled rooms
of their casita. Now, as shadows form outside, they hear
the luxury of water flowing down their driveway, draining
through the gutters, evaporating in a silent whisper
on the streets. California. California.

## The Cathedral of Girona

*"a baptism of dark water" -Lorca*

Tourist, traveler, I enter the cathedral from the busy square,
from the *bodega* where we have just eaten *boquerones*, crusty
bread, drunk a glass of wine. I climb the steps in silence one
by one, pass through the wooden door. inhale the texture of
the darkness, the tapestry of worn air: nine hundred years
of whispered sighs and supplications. *Mea Culpa. Mea Culpa.*
On the cool hard floor, the stones are smooth and worn by the
need of the pious to confess, by their yearning for paradise.
To the side of the altar stand the choir stalls that one family
carved for a century. *Dei gloria.* The patina of the wood is still
stained with sin. Near me, in a pew, an old woman fingers beads
before a bank of flickering candles. She has been here for centuries.
As I turn toward her, tourist, traveler, I see my grandfather sitting
silent on a plain wooden bench below the lustrous silver *reredo.*
He moves over as I approach and makes room.

# A Change of Seasons in the Sierra

Black clouds forming over Dodge Ridge this morning:
late June and the irony of early summer rainfall,
untimely, as the dog and I move through the trees.
Dry shafts of snow plants are dull in the meadow grass.
Clumps of yellow iris fade on the forest floor,
heads drooping, flat leaves showing brown at the tips.
Among the bones of fallen trees,the dog noses scattered
feathers, a bird caught by the rush of a sudden owl.

To the west, in a hospital bed two hundred miles away,
my friend lies dying, her hair a pale yellow on the pillow.
What consumes her is the insatiable love that nature holds,
the embrace of mortality, the steady passion that pulls us,
inevitably, into a pervasive aura enfolding the earth,
limitless as the purple spread of lupine across the Sierra,
dense as the mist which envelops the dog and me
as we walk on, closer each step, each moment to her.

Remember, friend, that dying begins with our first breath.
Seconds, minutes, cells trickle slowly, imperceptively away,
down to the sea, like Strawberry Creek in midsummer.
But a fresh torrent will rush through the canyon each spring.
Birds and buds will emerge from the chill death of winter,
the jays will move in a blue flutter through the trees, and the
snow plants in May will thrust passionately through the soil.
In pools of sunlight, the slender iris will sway in the meadow.

## Deadfalls

*for my mother*

In the worst places there are none:
trees logged, slash cut, the scarred
ground cleared, debris dragged away,
new seedlings planted. Forest Science.
Occasionally, in the foothills or the
deep unmanaged forests you will find them:
scarred by lightning, sapped by disease,
finally windswept to the ground, erupted
roots flung higher than the fallen trunk.
Then the carpenter ants and termites
begin their work, scavenging, cleaning
the skeleton, white fingers of limbs stark
against the brown grasses and pine needles.
Then the bulk of the tree settles slowly,
season by season into the rain-softened ground
and returns to the earth.

When you see these deadfalls, you will know
the form that death should follow: jagged bolt
in a weakened heart, last fall in a familiar place,
then the years gradually erasing the memories.
Finally, the communion with all fallen lives and
the aura of the earth.

# De Rerum Natura

*for Joe*

You seem to have been walking forever,
beyond those trees, beyond that creek,
even beyond where the washed blue sky
meets the mountains. You travel light,
just the backpack holding to your body.
You have gorp, a hand lens, binoculars,
a well-thumbed field guide. You stop
along the path, call birds out of the sky,
rub the leaves of alpine laurel in your fingers,
allow the smell to deepen in your lungs.
You know all this, like Lucretius, at home
in this terrain of thought. Later in the day,
you leave the trail and make your way
to the creek, kneel down to drink, take off
boots and socks, stretch out on the sand bar,
let the dampness cool your feet. The wonder
of water. From under your hat, you look at
forms of grey stone slabs, a stand of pine trees,
slope and sky. You rest between uncertainties.

# Diversity

We took the road which winds up from Torremolinos,
above the impersonal luxury of the Hotel Pyramides,
beyond the indolence of the topless beaches on the coast,
and made our way to Benalmadena, without a thought
other than to leave the English tourists, the fast-food places,
the fervid shopkeepers behind.

In the village, we found
a room in a hostel. *Semana Sancta* and even here the
inns were full. Three beds for two children and ourselves.
One bathroom, shared with a man who coughed, smoked
and spat through the night: a woman who took possession
early in the morning and refused to leave.

That first night
we went out on the street to see the *pasos* carried through
the narrow, winding alleys to the plaza. Leading the crowd,
with a pole to lift electric wires so the saints could pass
beneath, was the nephew of the mayor, a bent and foolish
figure who was often careless, distracted by the laughter,
and then the sparks would fly.

# Faces in Siena

1.

The women of fashion in Siena
step through the ancient alleys
of the city, their faces flawless,
skin and flesh unwrinkled, tucked
and tightened in expensive clinics,
all signs of sorrow smoothed away,
the mottled years absolved and gone.

2.

The walls around the piazza in Siena
are formed of yellowed stone, their
faces streaked by ancient stains, the
water wrinkling the time-worn surface.
Occasionally, a subtle smear of ochre
deep in the weathered limestone, like
a faded memory of happiness or grief.

# Bodega Harbor

The last light hangs on the eastern hills,
as the buoy moans its muffled warning;
the boat channel is still in the twilight.
We walk quietly, pensively down the road,
following the curve of the bay, looking back
occasionally, solemnly, at the red glow
in the west, the sun going down on Bodega
harbor, on us all.

Near a sand bar washed by small waves,
a noisy crowd of godwits floats like chum
on the darkening water. In random confusion
they rise in the air, fall back to the shifting
sand, circling carelessly, clamoring against
the quiet, ordered evening with raucous cries.
They stir as we approach, wings opening,
then closing, flying off, wheeling in the air.
Finally the whole flock moves fast above the water,
seeking a more insular shore.

Close by, untroubled by the rush, stands
a solitary egret, white as truth, an archive of light,
almost luminescent as night enfolds the world.
In the twilight, our eyes are held by the egret.

# First

Imagine losing your virginity
at Pyramid Lake in the desert
outside Reno, Nevada, the night
so dark that the spires of tufa
rising from the darkling lake
light the moonscape beach
and the awkward thrust and flare
of your random and wild young
bodies.

Imagine catching the Lahontan
trout, maybe twenty pounds, on
fifteen test: the tentative yet
forceful strike, then the struggle,
the line paying out, the falling
of spirit when the fish makes its run.
Then it pulls again, and you know
you haven't lost what you didn't
know you had.

# Fishing with my Father

Such a glow on the lake with dark descending:
sun on the granite slopes but growing shadows,
not a whisper of wind in the trees to stir the water.
The twilight, my father felt, was best for fishing,
that mysterious margin between day and night,
so we'd stand on the dock together, trout rising
lazily through the lush green surface of the lake,
casting our lines, reeling in, careful with words.
It took me years and children to know what we
we fished for in that silence. Then, I was young,
wanting only the rapture of the strike, the trout
arching its back on the dock, but my father threw
his lure again and again, until there was no light.

# A Journey in Provence

My body drowsy
after making love this morning,
slow to move into the day.
I listen at the table
while friends make plans:
what roads to take,
what villages to visit.

Earlier, my love, we lost ourselves
in twisting but familiar streets
and found ourselves at a fountain,
in a plaza, by a church.
We made our way together,
found the stillness in the sanctuary,
then we lit a candle.

Always, in the miracle that is love,
we light a candle to flicker in that holy space
for our return.

# In September, in France

In the countryside
around Le Tour,
still scarred by war,
the morning sun
first lights the topmost
branches of the trees.

No sound except
the calls of birds,
the cooing of a dove,
the air still cool
and motionless
inside the courtyard.

Then sharp explosions,
as hunters consecrate
the ritual opening of
another season, dark
blood thick on leaves.

# Los Milagros

Early morning in Cuernavaca,
the pale sun pouring into the city
from over the eastern hills and slowly
filling the streets, the alleys, the plaza
which fronts the *Edificio de Sud America,*
where a woman prepares her *tortillas,*
*hecho a mano* and cooked on her knees
in the gutter on a grill to be sold.

She has arrived on the bus, goes back
on the bus to a *pueblo* hidden in the hills.
Here she pats out the *masa*, heats it on
the grill and offers it to a man in a suit
who hands her some *pesetas*, and he tears
the *tortilla*, this wafer of corn soaked in
water, puts a piece on his tongue, tastes
the earth of his birthplace and more,

sees a vision of himself playing soccer
near the plaza with a ball made of rags
in the midst of a mud-splattered crowd
of children who are shouting and running
toward a dotcom dream they have stood
in the street to see on TV, the big screen
shining in the storefront, even while the
dark *aguacero* fills the gutters each day.

# Morning in Oaxaca

Early morning outside the hotel in Oaxaca,
such ominous light in the washed gray sky,
the street quiet, row after row of colonial houses.
I was just eighteen, on holiday with my parents,
when I stepped out the door, looking for life.
What could I know of the sleeping city, the wealthy
people living behind shutters and walls? As I walked,
I would glance through heavy gates and glimpse
the bougainvillea staining the whitewashed houses.
I must have walked miles, past the *zocalo,* the market
where a pickup filled with bloody cow heads blinded me.
I was looking for love, poetry glistening in my eyes,
so it took me years to know what I had found instead,
years to taste a soup in which a cow head simmered for
hours with onions and garlic, beans and some herbs,
a soup to hold a man who plows a barren pasture,
who fucks a woman nightly in a loveless marriage,
fathers a brood of surly children and feeds them, never
knowing that they will live in a poem which will be strained
then sipped years later on a sunny afternoon in California.

# Mozart in the Mountains

Outside the windows,
the earth is still and white,
snow everywhere,
even dusting the black rocks
where the small creek lies.
But the stillness is deceptive.
Beneath the snow a thaw begins,
tiny crystals of ice releasing their form
to the ground, then to rivulets,
and the slowly swelling creek,
then to the river and down to the sea.
Even as you sense this dance of water,
look upward to the icy slopes---
sun glistening on that glacier.
The music of that water held for centuries.

# Sabicas in Assisi

In the Grand Hotel Subasio, in Assisi, in September:
frayed carpets, noisy plumbing, a faded counterpane
on the stately, sagging bed. Then the porter opened
the wooden shutters and below us was the Umbrian
Plain, a patch of yellow, green and sorrel fields
with roads and lanes leading up to hills still gold
in evening sunlight.

Jesus, what a view, we said
then tipped the porter and wandered out to see the city:
narrow streets, a sprawl of shops all selling coffee mugs
or statuettes or tee shirts with the image of the saint,
lion and lamb at his feet, birds settled on his head and
outstretched arms: a homespun robe and sandals,
Francis: poverty and peace.

We found Sabicas in a bar,
just off the street that leads up to the cathedral, smearing
wine drops on the table in senseless whorls. He's drunk,
of course, this god of gypsy music, numb with rage, and
muttering about revenge and death: the snarl of men below
the walls, the keening women, iron slashes, bloodstained
clods of fresh-turned earth.

In every patch of ground
where people meet and pray the vision Francis lived,
the fields seem a harmony of color, and roads lead up to
hills of grass in a golden shower of sunlight. Elsewhere,
passion still persists, and peace remains elusive: the heavy
smell of vengeance in the air, proud flesh, a throbbing scar
when rain falls and the *duende*.

In darkness, later,
in our room, we sat with shutters open and watched
the storm invading Umbria: loud thunder, shafts of lightning,
then a smell of cordite heavy in the air, and the clouds moved
purple to the east like massive bruises. Toward Kosovo,
toward Serbia, toward Sarjevo. When the wind became
relentless, we went to bed
and held each other close.

# San Felipe

After the wreckage of the marriage,
there was still a little money,
so I went alone to San Felipe,
to a small motel behind the beach,
ate prawns *al ajo* in a cheap cantina,
slept drunk each night on dirty sheets
and walked the morning sand, a nail
of tequila pulsing in my temples.
The Sea of Cortez stretched for miles,
empty ocean, empty sky, and I struggled
with the weight of failure.
                                        When you fail
at what you once called love, your senses
turn to stone. You look out to the horizon
but cannot see the line between blue water
and blue sky; the order of the world is gone.
Across the Gulf of California, turtles swim
for miles to lay their eggs on beaches they
are destined for, and some do not survive.
But I was lucky. By chance I found a seashell
waiting in the sand, and in my ear I heard
the welcoming ocean.

# Travel

In the courtyard of the rented flat in Rue Suger,
sparrows flew from one small window box to
another in an open shaft of humdrum air, rising
and diving in that quiet space past hewn stone
walls, then lighting for a moment in the red geraniums.

# Two Lakes in Italy and Encimer

Lago de Garda in the early evening, last light draining
into mist-shrouded water and the form of the faraway
shore like a partly recovered memory: the low land
dark and dense through wisps of fog in the distance.
We stayed at the Fiordaliso, an elegant villa Mussolini
procured for his mistress when his stiff-armed salute
and upthrust chin made fascist Italy his other possession.
Under the pier, as we sipped our wine, a school of sardines
made their way through the crystal waters and later we dined
in a damask-draped room on the self-same fish, now finished
in a tasteful sauce.

Lago de Como: the Hotel Loveno, far above Menaggio, high
in the unfashionable hills above the resorts and grand hotels.
A high-ceilinged room with a faded patina on the wainscotting,
wheezing registers, the sound of cars crawling uphill in the rain.
There was no view, and I sat in the darkness while you bathed,
drinking wine and thinking of Encimer, his rented room in Berkeley,
his exile from university, the writer of our generation we thought,
artist and the bohemian we could not allow ourselves to be.
He wound up in a bookstore, the novel never finished, living out
his years, while Mussolini, with Claretta, was stopped in Dunga,
dragged from the car and hanged by a crowd who relished in
the flavor of that fall.

# Who Can Know the Desert?

*for Sage, 1977*

It has always been so, Sage.
The desert lies like an ancient bone,
picked clean by birds, a place of sand and silence
where greed, ambition and careless affluence cannot survive.
In the desert you will live without the shade of trees,
without the fragile lovliness of flowers. Your only music
will be the wind, winding down the dunes and canyons.

But when thunder flattens the herd of sheep,
when lightning quickens the lizard's blood,
You will move away from the comforting fire, fearless,
and watch the dawn.

## Writing the Sierra Winter

1
Each morning in the winter I take a long walk
through the meadow down to where I think
the wandering beds of two small creeks
might finally merge.

2
The darkling bands of water trickle through
some scattered stones, by fallen branches,
unseen below the crusted snow, some mornings
frozen when the cold snaps hard and holds.

3
Others also tramp this meadow, always another's
way worn smooth, but I make my own steps,
sometimes stagger through the crust and flounder
like a drunkard in the drifts.

4
If, in my walking, I see ahead a clump of buck brush,
holding early sunlight, fragile as a cloud of frozen breath,
rising from the creekhead near the dense green pines
that stretch below the snow-swept mountain,

5
I am home.

# ABOUT THE AUTHOR

**Paul Neumann** was born and raised on the coast of California. For the past forty-three years he has made his home in Modesto. He traveled extensively in the 80's and 90's, but his work since then has been centered on the Central Valley and the people who live and work there. His first book, *Forms of Light,* was published by Quercus Review Press in 2003.

www.ingramcontent.com/pod-product-compliance
Lightning Source LLC
LaVergne TN
LVHW091011080826
845145LV00003B/1229

*9780615873312*